Give Bees a Chance

written and illustrated by

Alicia Previn

published by

Lovely Previn Publications

TortoiseBrand Books

Contents

ISBN 978-0-9847107-2-0

Where does your food come from?

Are you hungry? Imagine your favorite things to eat. The whole world is a very big place with millions and billions of people who are also very, very hungry. We go to a market or a restaurant to buy food that is grown and produced by farmers from the wide areas in the world that have good growing conditions. There are lots of hungry mouths to feed so the farmers try to grow as much as they can, which means fields are full of plants as far as the eye can see. Plants need to be fed too. They need some of the same things we need to live, like water, food, sunshine, air, and friends like the friendly creatures that help them grow.

From seed to flower

Did you know that a plant begins as a seed? A big yellow sunflower comes from the tiny seeds that grow in the middle. Just like the seeds of apples, grapes, tomatoes, corn, nuts, and many vegetables, even plants that make the fabric for the clothes you wear. The soil that the seeds are planted in must be full of life-giving food for the plant to sprout, grow leaves and eventually a flower comes that opens its petals.

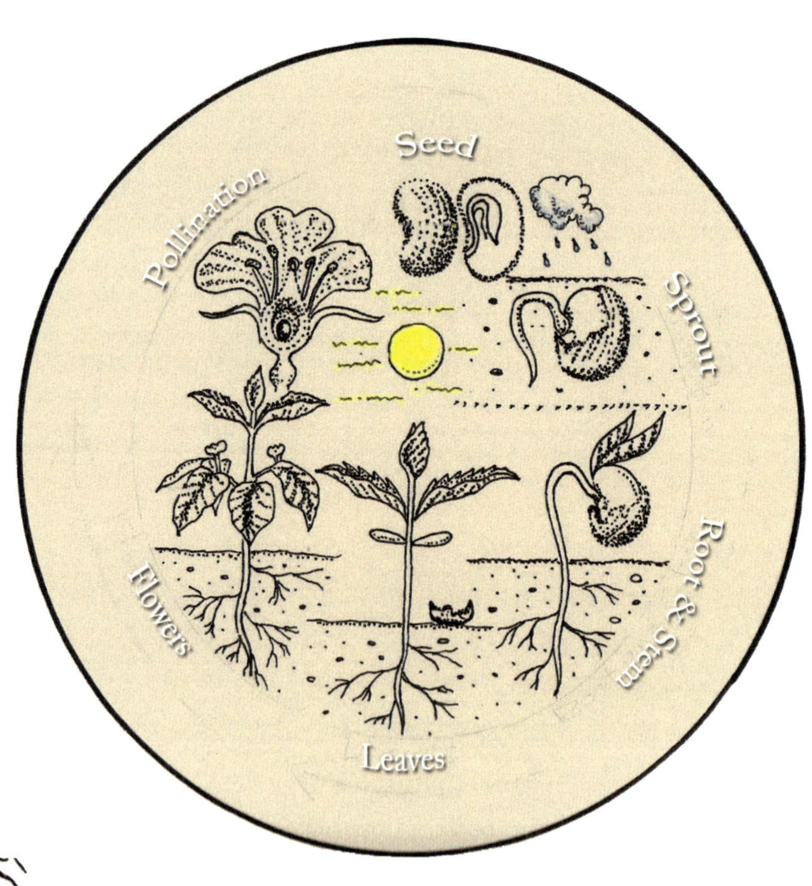

The flowers are brightly colored or have an aroma that attracts friendly flying creatures inside to drink their sweet nectar, then by collecting it from many blooms in one day they fly home to deliver it to feed their family.

What is pollination and how does it work?

While bees are drinking inside the flower, there are parts of the flower covered with golden powder that touch the bees and it sticks on their bodies. This powder is called pollen and it has information about the plant that needs to be shared. This is an easy task for bees to cooperate with the plants, because each time a bee goes to visit another flower to drink, it keeps exchanging information by bringing the pollen from flower to flower.

Flower to fruit

The shared pollen transforms the flowers into food-producing plants that will also make new seeds so we can continue to plant and eat.

We need Bees to live

Think about that for a second! Look at how nature works perfectly together in harmony and everything gets what they need. Without the important help of the bees (and some butterflies too) buzzing and fluttering around all day, this wonderful cycle of growing and sharing to make food would stop. We need bees to live.

Bees' home and hive

A bee's home is called a hive and is made of many tiny holes or rooms that have eight sides or walls, all made of wax. Inside, the worker bees place the nectar and cover each hole with more wax. Most important of all in the hive is the queen bee, who is larger and longer than other bees. She is busy all day laying eggs inside the rooms, which will eventually become baby bees.

Give Bees a Chance

Once the nectar is put inside the wax-covered holes and stored for food we call it honeycomb. Honey is golden, sticky, sweet and a very healthful food that bees share with us. To make just one small spoonful means a whole life's work for 12 bees. Bees have an amazing waggle dance they perform for the other bees in the hive to show them exactly where the nectar and pollen are.

Watch it here and try the bee dance:

Place your QR code scanner reader here

CLICK button below to open
Give Bees A Chance video
only for ebook version

They don't want to hurt you

Bees can be scary when they're buzzing around, but if you think about how small they are and how big you are, then you can understand that they can get scared if you start waving your hands around and screaming. The best thing you can do is to stand very still, be calm and then walk slowly away.
They do not want to hurt you.

Bees are in big trouble

The bees help us and share with us, so we need to care for them, and they're in big trouble. When bees are in trouble that is like a sign warning us that we must stop what we are doing and fix what is going wrong. There are many things making them sick, even the food they are pollinating is not healthy and can have diseases. The air and water around them are hurting them, as many farmers are spraying chemical poisons on the huge fields of plants to keep off bugs that eat and spoil the crops they sell to our markets. The chemicals also take the life out of the ground, and we now know plants need this to grow strong and be good for our food to nourish us so we too can be heal.

How can one person make a difference?

This problem has spread all across the world. We may wonder, how can one little person make a difference for saving the bees? Everyone can do their part to create bee sanctuaries; a sanctuary is a place you can go where it is safe and pure, where nothing can harm you.

Help the plants stay healthy

Right in our own yard we can plant bee-friendly flowers, but we promise to not use any weed killers or chemicals. Weeding by hand is a very important job. The very best we can do for our garden is to give it compost and make an earthworm box (see how in back of The Earthworm Book) to help the plants stay healthy and use a natural rich soil,* which makes sure plants have more sweetness and nutrients. Bees want go out and gather nectar, but if the food is not healthy and sweet, they won't fly. Just like us they like food that tastes good! We want them to be healthy, enjoying their beautiful work and loving their families.

* the NutrientRich© program See MicroSoil™.com

MicroSoil and the NutrientRich program

THE SOLUTION: Create a MicroSoil® " Bee Haven™"

1. Get rid of chemical fertilizers
2. Develop a farming and fertilization program of natural occurring nutrients, such as our MicroSoil® Nutrient Package.
3. MicroSoil® puts LIFE back into your soils, which puts LIFE, higher BRIX, and higher nutrient values into the plants, which pass along these attributes to the bees and into the plants and fruits for all to enjoy.
4. If you will build healthy nutrient rich soils for your crops all else will follow in good order

"THIS IS, AND HAS BEEN, NATURE'S WAY SINCE THE BEGINNING OF TIME".

THE BENEFITS:

1. Increase in healthy bee populations
2. Increase in blossom sets
3. Increased pollination
4. Increase in quality and quantity in crop yields
5. Increase in soil energy and health
6. Increase in water retention in soils

MicroSoil® products, which have been sold worldwide for over 15 years, utilizes ONLY natural Synergistic Catalysts and nature's irrefutable natural occurring nutrients, processes and rhythms in its formulas.

Give Bees a Chance Song Lyrics

© song & lyrics by Alicia Previn

Buzz buzz buzz buzz....
Honey honey honey honey....
Flower pollen
flower pollen
Give Bees a Chance, We need them!
Please Save the Bees!
A flower blooms and opens wide
For buzzing bees to crawl inside
Drinking nectar from the cups
Tickled by their golden dust
Flying inside many blooms
Homeward to 8 sided rooms
Give Bees a Chance, We need them to Live
Bees love to dance Please Save the Bees!
Watch to see those plants are pure
We want no harm to come to you
Poison to the hive and queen
Dying bees is what we've seen
Bees are friends with honey to share
They only sting when they are scared
So be very still
Give Bees a Chance, We need them
Please Save the Bees!

Thank you Don D. Haller for comissioning this book, but more importantly for creating the Nutrient Rich© (products) solution to the problem and for his love for all the friendly creatures.
Many million thanks to Claudia Previn Stasny for her editing, expertise, creativity and knowledge about the programs that assisted me in creating the illustrations and book formatting.

Visit the Lovely Previn Publications website for more about TortoiseBrand Books
www.AliciaPrevin.com
Facebook.com/GiveBeesAChanceSong

The following 3 pages are in black and white for you to COLOR any way you like! Enjoy...

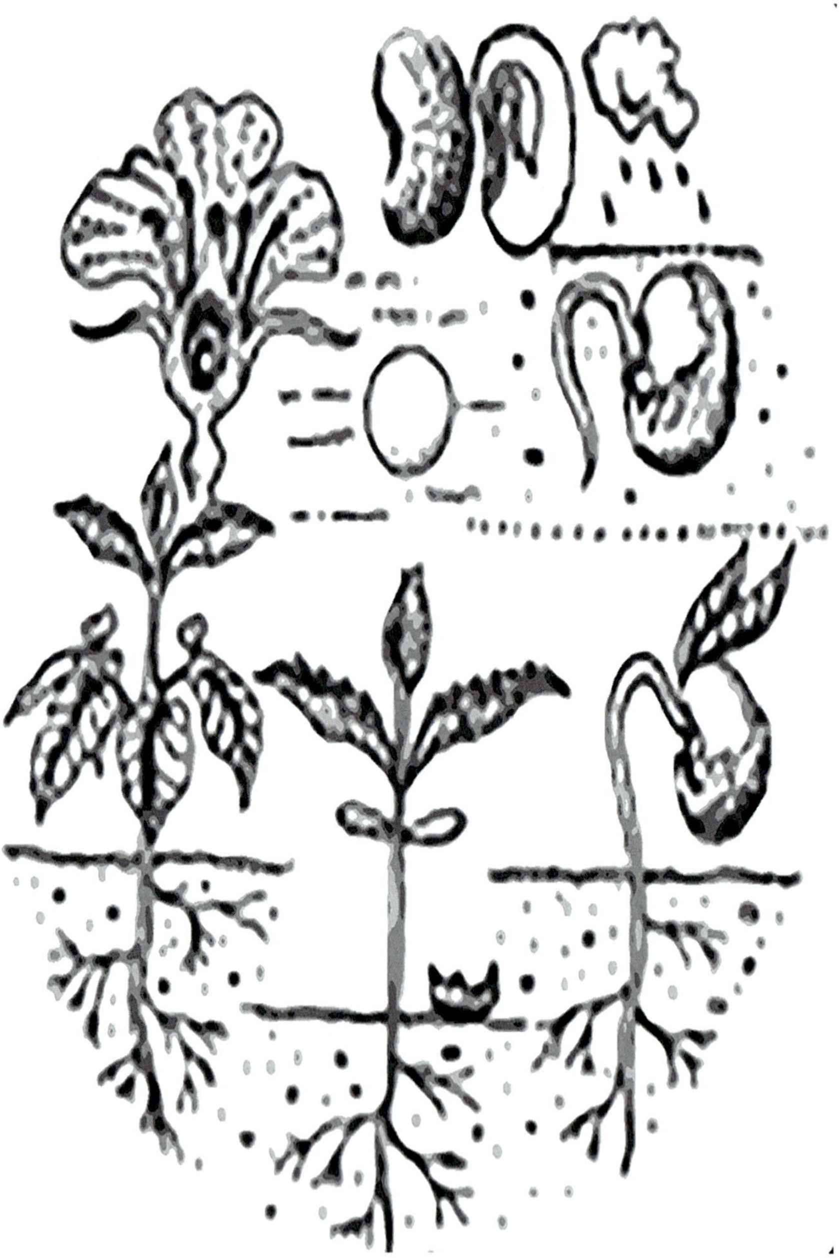

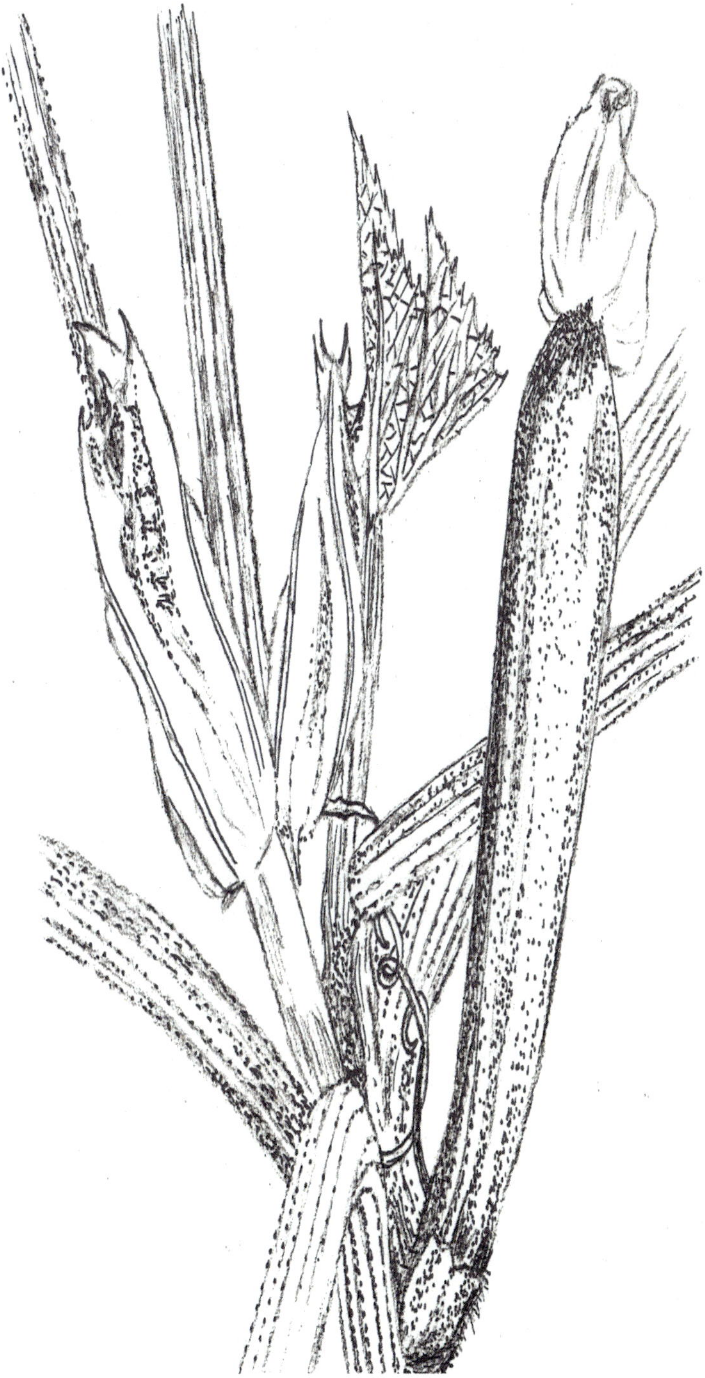

BEE
BYE BYE!

Made in the USA
Coppell, TX
20 January 2026